REACHING THE SUSTAINABLE DEVELOPMENT GOALS THROUGH BETTER LOCAL-LEVEL DATA

A CASE STUDY ON LUMAJANG AND PACITAN DISTRICTS IN INDONESIA

OCTOBER 2020

ASIAN DEVELOPMENT BANK

ADB

Contents

FIGURES   iv

ACKNOWLEDGMENTS   v

ABBREVIATIONS   vi

KEY POINTS   vii

INTRODUCTION   1

THE SUSTAINABLE DEVELOPMENT GOALS AT THE LOCAL LEVEL   2
    Local Governments Cannot Achieve This Alone   2
    Good Data are Key to Localizing the Sustainable Development Goals   3
    Local Data are Not Always Readily Available   3

LOCALIZING THE SUSTAINABLE DEVELOPMENT GOALS:
THE EXAMPLE OF EAST JAVA, INDONESIA   5
    Advancing Localization of Sustainable Development Goals in Indonesia   5
    Enhancing Data Access and Utilization in East Java   7
    Leveraging Data Visualization Tools to Inform Local Policy Dialogues
       and Sustainable Development Goals Localization   8
    A Locally Owned Process for Data Visualization   8
    The Indicator Framework Development   9
    Data Mapping and Compilation   11
    Dashboard Development   13

DASHBOARD USE AND LAUNCH   16
    Capacity Development for Multiple Stakeholders for Sustainability   16

STRENGTHENING LOCAL CROSS-SECTOR POLICY DIALOGUE   17

HOW PRESENTING THE DATA LED TO CHANGE   19

NEXT STEPS AND LESSONS LEARNED   21
    Next Steps   21
    Lessons Learned   21

Figures

1   Progress in the Four Areas to Localize the Sustainable Development Goals Requires Access to Data   3

2   The Leadership, Ownership, and Capacities for Agenda 2030 Local Implementation
     and Stakeholders Empowerment Sustainable Development Goals Project in Indonesia   6

3   Six-Step Over-all Dashboard Development Process   9

4   Girls Not Brides Framework to Tackle Child Marriage   10

5   Simplified Indicator Framework for Ending Child Marriage   11

6   Dashboard Data Map and Management   12

7   Child Marriage Dashboard Examples   13

8   Working Toward Policy Coherence Across Sectors   18

Acknowledgments

AUTHORS:

Kirthi Ramesh is a social sector specialist, Central and West Asia Department, Asian Development Bank (ADB).

Rosebelle May Azcuna is an independent monitoring and evaluation expert.

Susann Roth is a principal knowledge sharing and services specialist, Knowledge Advisory Service Center of ADB.

Dina Limanto is an open government specialist at ADB.

Jane Parry is an independent consultant and public health communications expert.

Ruchita Rajbhandary is a consultant data analytics expert.

The authors would like to express their profound thanks to the dashboard development teams of the local governments in East Java Province, Kab. Lumajang, and Kab. Pacitan as well as local nongovernment stakeholders, Anton Baare, Claudia Buentjen, Francesca Francavilla, Mark Landry, Keiko R. Nowacka, Ping Nugrawira, Azusa Sato, Sukarni, Paulus Suprayitno, Muholizah Utami, Kate Walton, and Winfried Wicklein.

Abbreviations

ADB   Asian Development Bank

SDGs   Sustainable Development Goals

Key Points

- The Sustainable Development Goals (SDGs) set global, big-picture targets that nations have committed to attaining. However, unless action is taken at the local level, these targets can never be reached.

- Localizing the SDGs entails a process of defining, implementing, and monitoring local-level strategies to reach global, national, and subnational targets. While local governments are often responsible for delivering health, education, and social services, they can only achieve the localization of the SDGs in collaboration with other stakeholders.

- Access to good data supports implementation of SDGs by providing evidence to enable better planning, budgeting, and implementation. As development outcomes can vary widely from one locality to the next, the more granular and geographically disaggregated the data is, the more policies and programs can be tailored to the needs of local communities.

- In Indonesia, decentralization has opened a window of opportunity for subnational governments to take a stronger role in implementing SDGs at the local level.

- The Asian Development Bank worked with local governments and other stakeholders in East Java to make data from districts available and accessible in a visually attractive and easy-to-understand way for different local stakeholders, thereby contributing to localizing SDGs.

- One of the identified issues in East Java that constrains achieving the social development related SDGs is child marriage. It can only be successfully tackled using genuinely intersector, local solutions. This issue was chosen as proof of concept of local dashboards to improve access to information and inform local policy dialogues.

- Creating dashboards was a highly consultative process, giving participants the language and conceptual framework to have conversations with each other about a cross-sector issue. The dashboards helped identify the indicators and related data where they each need to take action.

- Several new policy recommendations emerged from using the dashboards and district governments in East Java are now considering using dashboards for other indicators, such as education of out-of-school-youth, and in other sectors. The local governments demonstrated a high level of ownership even after the project ended. With the onset of the coronavirus disease (COVID-19) pandemic, local governments used their newly acquired skills to create dashboards to monitor the pandemic in their constituencies.

Introduction

The Sustainable Development Goals (SDGs) set global, big-picture targets that nations have committed to attaining. However, unless action is taken at the local level to implement them and monitor progress toward their targets, these goals can never be reached. Localizing the SDGs is a pressing task worldwide, even among the developing member countries of the Asian Development Bank (ADB).

Countries know that they must effectively localize the SDGs, because of their mixed experiences of trying to do so with its predecessor, the Millennium Development Goals. One of the key weaknesses that undermined the achievement of Millennium Development Goals' targets was local stakeholders' lack of capacity and ownership, missing an opportunity to reach more targeted populations.[1] For ADB, learning from these lessons meant that *Strategy 2030*,[2] a road map to respond effectively to the region's changing needs, includes a commitment to localization of the SDGs.[3] This means supporting local governments and other local stakeholders in monitoring, implementing, raising awareness, and advocating for the SDGs.[4]

---

[1] ADB. 2018. *Localizing the Sustainable Development Goals to Accelerate Implementation of the 2030 Agenda for Sustainable Development. The Current State of Sustainable Development Goal Localization in Asia and the Pacific.* Manila. https://www.adb.org/sites/default/files/publication/472021/governance-brief-033-sdgs-implementation-2030-agenda.pdf.

[2] ADB. 2018. *Strategy 2030: Achieving a Prosperous, Inclusive, Resilient, and Sustainable Asia and the Pacific.* Manila. https://www.adb.org/documents/strategy-2030-prosperous-inclusive-resilient-sustainable-asia-pacific.

[3] ADB. 2019. *Operational Priority 6: Strengthening Governance and Institutional Capacity.* Manila. https://www.adb.org/sites/default/files/institutional-document/495976/strategy-2030-op6-governance.pdf.

[4] Fernández de Losada A. *Localizing the Post-2015 Development Agenda Dialogues on Implementation.* United Nations Development Programme and United Nations Human Settlements Programme.https://www.uclg.org/sites/default/files/dialogues_on_localizing_the_post-2015_development_agenda.pdf.

The Sustainable Development Goals at the Local Level

Localizing the SDGs entails a process of firstly defining local-level strategies to reach national, and subnational targets of global goals, then implementing and monitoring those strategies. This requires concrete mechanisms, platforms, and processes and clear accountability that can effectively translate the development agenda into results at the local level (footnote 4).

Localizing the SDG agenda is also key to "leaving no one behind."[5] People get left behind in social development due to discrimination, geography, governance, socioeconomic status, and external shocks or state fragility. Those left behind typically contend with intersecting disadvantages, and evidence suggests that those most likely to be left behind are women and girls in rural areas born to poor families and belonging to a minority ethnic group (footnote 5). Only a holistic response that transcends sector silos can effectively overcome these interwoven disadvantages.

Local Governments Cannot Achieve This Alone

In many countries, in particular those with decentralized government structures, local governments are responsible for delivering many health, education, and social services. Lower levels of government are closer to local communities and can therefore be more responsive to local needs. The SDGs at the same time provide local governments a framework for local development. However, local governments cannot achieve the localization of the SDGs on their own. Civil society, traditional leaders, religious organizations, academia, and private sector actors all play a key role in this process (footnote 5).

In its *Roadmap for Localizing SDGs: Implementation and Monitoring at Subnational Level,*[6] the United Nations outlines four key areas:

1. **Awareness raising.** Local governments play an important role in raising local awareness and ownership of the SDG agenda through various tools including traditional and social media, campaigns, and formal and informal education.

2. **Advocacy.** Localizing SDGs can reinforce multilevel governance and facilitate the participation of local governments in development of national SDG strategies.

3. **Implementation.** Local governments can prepare to implement SDGs in their communities by conducting a needs assessment to define priorities, aligning local development plans with SDGs, and mobilizing local resources and leadership capacity.

4. **Monitoring.** Information gathered at local level should be used in national monitoring and reporting for the 231 SDG indicators. In turn, the SDG indicators should be used to monitor and review local plans and ensure local achievements are recognized as part of the national SDG progress reports.

5   UNDP. 2018. *What Does It Mean to Leave No One Behind? A UNDP Discussion Paper and Framework for Implementation.* https://www.undp.org/content/dam/undp/library/Sustainable%20Development/2030%20Agenda/Discussion_Paper_LNOB_EN_lres.pdf.
6   Global Taskforce of Local and Regional Governments, UNDP, UN-Habitat. 2016. *Roadmap for Localizing the SDGs: Implementation and Monitoring at Subnational Level.* Barcelona. https://sustainabledevelopment.un.org/content/documents/commitments/818_11195_commitment_ROADMAP%20LOCALIZING%20SDGS.pdf.

Good Data are Key to Localizing the Sustainable Development Goals

A key requirement to localizing SDGs is the availability of and access to local data. Armed with this powerful data, it is possible to raise awareness on the progress of SDGs among local governments and communities, draw attention to where the greatest needs are, advocate for the required resources and capacity, and have a say in national SDG strategies. Access to good data supports implementation of SDGs by enabling better planning, budgeting, and implementation.

Given that development outcomes can vary widely from one locality to the next, the more granular and geographically disaggregated the data is, the more policies and programs can be tailored to the needs of local communities. Data can be the catalyst that engages various segments of society in localizing the SDG agenda. Data can be strategically used by local governments to improve service delivery, monitor development indicators, and inform policy and decision-making. They can support civil society to engage in constructive dialogue with governments, provide feedback, and hold local governments accountable. Academia, journalists, and other stakeholders also benefit from access to good data.

Local Data are Not Always Readily Available

Despite their importance, quality, relevant, and timely local data are not always readily available. This can be for a variety of reasons, including poorly defined indicators, fragmentation across various sources, and inefficient data collection, which makes it difficult to collate and share data (such as on paper or through discrete databases). The burden of data collection typically falls on frontline staff, such as health workers, taking them away from their main responsibilities. Whatever data collected may also be of dubious quality, with duplications, irregular updates, and insufficient disaggregation. Data privacy is another key concern.

Another layer of challenges lies in data use. Data may not be used effectively because they are not relevant for decision-making or because of users' low data literacy. Data may be complete but are directly channeled to the national level and inaccessible at the local level.

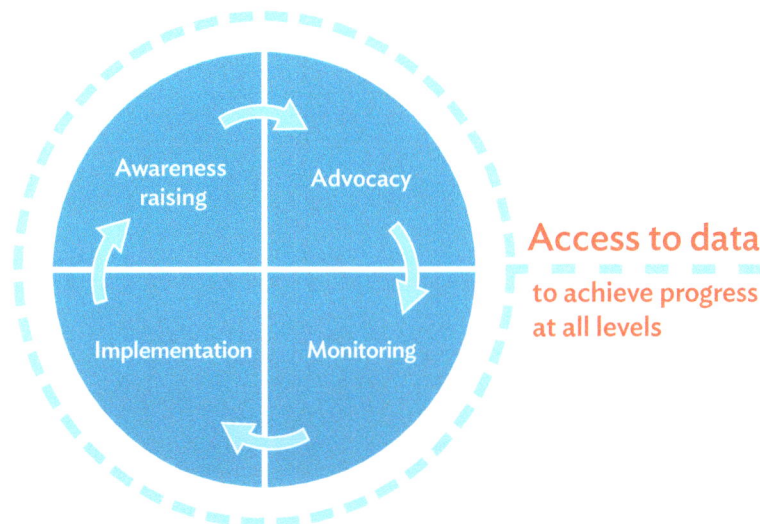

Figure 1: Progress in the Four Areas to Localize the Sustainable Development Goals Requires Access to Data

Awareness raising

Advocacy

Implementation

Monitoring

Access to data
to achieve progress
at all levels

Source: Authors, adapted from Global Taskforce of Local and Regional Governments, United Nations Development Programme, UN-Habitat. 2016.

For the public, data are not always available and where they are, may be limited to basic information, and exclude metrics on performance and progress. Even where freedom of information legislation is in place, citizens may have to go through cumbersome procedures to request access to data. Thus, communities find it difficult to hold local governments accountable, or get information on the services and rights to which they are entitled. Lack of usage may in turn further exacerbate weak data quality and relevance. Moreover, making data available is not enough: the power of data is unleashed when it is combined with other methods to bring about change.[7]

[7] UNDP Eurasia. 2020. A New Year, New Perspectives on Data Innovation. *Medium*. 7 January. https://medium.com/innovation-in-the-age-of-the-sustainable- developme/a-new-year-new-perspectives-on-data-innovation-dd740fac880d.

Localizing the Sustainable Development Goals: The Example of East Java, Indonesia

Advancing Localization of Sustainable Development Goals in Indonesia

In 2000, Indonesia embarked on far-reaching decentralization reforms, granting a substantial degree of political and fiscal autonomy to subnational governments, including for delivery of services such as health and education. These reforms have opened a window of opportunity for subnational governments to take a stronger role in implementing SDGs at the local level.

To foster coherence of national and local policies for SDG implementation, a 2017 presidential decree formally required the integration of the SDGs and the national medium-term development plan into medium-term regional and local plans. It also called for the preparation of an SDG road map and several action plans, annual reports, and biannual monitoring systems at the subnational level.[8]

To support the localization of the SDGs, the government has also developed a specific communication strategy, a series of technical guidelines, a support system, and a set of metadata indicators—developed as part of the provincial and local government's vertical reporting process—to ensure buy-in by subnational levels of government. Nineteen of Indonesia's 34 provinces have developed and then formalized their SDG action plans by official decree, while a further 15 are currently in the process of completing theirs. At the same time, provincial, district, and municipal planning agencies play a key role in coordinating the implementation of the SDGs. Certain pilot provinces, such as Riau, and innovative cities, including the capital Jakarta, have taken the lead and aligned their medium-term development plans with the SDGs.[9]

At the same time, in 2019, Indonesia published *A Roadmap of SDGs in Indonesia*, calling for systemic reforms across a wide range of policy areas, from public administration to good governance and the strengthening of the management capacity of the central government and line governments' ministries.[10]

Most local governments have not yet adopted national SDG targets and therefore have not integrated SDG indicators into their data collection systems. Some provinces are training for SDGs and as a result have started developing local indicators (footnote 1). However, a survey on the status of SDGs implementation conducted under the Leadership, Ownership, and Capacities for Agenda 2030 Local Implementation and Stakeholders Empowerment Project (Figure 2) concluded that the requested indicators, in many cases, do not match the available data (footnote 9).

---

[8] United Cities and Local Governments. 2018. *Towards the Localization of the SDGs. United Cities and Local Governments, Local and Regional Governments' Report to the 2018 HLPF 2nd Report.* https://www.gold.uclg.org/sites/default/files/Towards_the_Localization_of_the_SDGs.pdf.

[9] United Cities and Local Governments. 2019. *Towards the Localization of the SDGs. United Cities and Local Governments, Local and Regional Governments' Report to the 2019 HLPF 3rd Report.* Barcelona.

[10] Government of Indonesia, Ministry of National Development Planning/ National Development Planning Agency. 2019. Roadmap of SDGs Indonesia: A Highlight. https://www.unicef.org/indonesia/media/1626/file/Roadmap%20of%20SDGs.pdf.

Figure 2: The Leadership, Ownership, and Capacities for Agenda 2030 Local Implementation and Stakeholders Empowerment Sustainable Development Goals Project in Indonesia

Leadership, Ownership, and Capacities for Agenda 2030 Local Implementation and Stakeholders Empowerment is a joint project that was launched by UCLG ASPAC and the Association of Indonesian Municipalities (APEKSI) in the first quarter of 2018. It receives support from the EU.

Building on the Presidential Decree 59 of 2017, its objective is to support the local implementation of SDGs by strengthening the capacities of local governments and their associations to plan, implement, and monitor SDGs at the local level.

The project involves 30 local governments (16 provinces and 14 cities) and five LGAs [APEKSI, APKASI, APPSI, ADEKSI and ADKASI). It collaborates regularly with the National Development Planning Agency and the Ministry of Home Affairs.

The road map for localizing SDGs

- Set up local political commitment to achieve SDGs
- Baseline study and stakeholder mapping to match available institutional function and issues of SDGs
- Set up a local SDGs special task force to ensure well-coordinated approach
- Develop action plan according to city development agenda that match the SDGs
- Synchronize local and national development agendas
- Setting up business model to finance SDGs action plan as a platform for multisector and cross-cutting issue partnership
- Develop a monitoring and evaluation scheme as a basis for reporting progress
- Promote exchange of best practices and initiate local government cooperation

ADEKSI = Asosiasi DPRD Kota Seluruh Indonesia (Indonesian Municipal Councils Association); ADKASI = Asosiasi DPRD Kabupaten Seluruh Indonesia (Association of Regency Governments of Indonesia); APEKSI = Asosiasi Pemerintah Kota Seluruh Indonesia (Association of Indonesian Municipalities); APKASI = Asosiasi Pemerintah Kabupaten Seluruh Indonesia (Association of District Governments of Indonesia); APPSI = Asosiasi Pemerintah Provinsi Seluruh Indonesia (Association of Provincial Governments of Indonesia); EU = European Union; LGA = Local Government Associations; SDG = sustainable development goal; UCLG ASPAC = United Cities and Local Governments of Asia Pacific.

Source: United Cities and Local Governments. 2018. *Towards the Localization of the SDGs. United Cities and Local Governments, Local and Regional Governments' Report to the 2018 HLPF 2nd Report*. Barcelona. https://www.uclg.org/sites/default/files/towards_the_localization_of_the_sdgs.pdf.

Meanwhile progress has been made to make data accessible to the public for advocacy, awareness raising, implementation, and monitoring under the 2008 Public Information Disclosure Act.[11] Under the law, citizens can submit a formal data access request through the relevant public agency. The act also provides for a dedicated information management and documentation officer in each public agency. However, there is a general lack of standard data management practices across government agencies. Each agency is working in its own silo, developing its own data management practice, with a lack of a clear strategy for data sharing and collaboration.[12]

To address these challenges, in 2018, President Jokowi passed a presidential decree for Satu Data (One Data), which mandates that all datasets produced by government agencies in Indonesia comply with a common set of standards set by the data, and a supervisory institution to be founded under the decree. Through this policy, Indonesia is expected to have a common framework for data management, and guidelines for public institutions to reduce redundant efforts, improve data quality, interoperability and integration, and create standardized data licensing and formats. Allowing data exchange across ministries and levels of government can have several benefits. Policy makers can access the information they need to make better resource allocation decisions and monitor outcomes within the population, while citizens benefit from easier access to and oversight of services.

Indonesia is also part of the Open Government Partnership. This international initiative encourages governments to promote transparency, increase public participation, fight corruption, and harness new technologies to make government more open, effective, and accountable.[13] Several commitments stipulated in the National Action Plan, 2018–2020 support strengthening local government's openness, transparency, and accountability (e.g., commitments 2, 3, 5) and achieving SDGs.

Enhancing Data Access and Utilization in East Java

Local governments in East Java introduced a range of good governance reforms to enhance local accountability and transparency in service delivery through the ADB-funded Local Governance Service Improvement (Kinerja) project.[14] One tool introduced through the project was a complaint mechanism that collected people-centered data from feedback on health and education services. Survey results were analyzed and discussed in participatory multi-stakeholder forums with community leaders, village youth, religious youth, civil society organizations, universities, and the media. It became apparent that these discussions could be further enriched through use of data from the districts to give a more complete picture of local development issues and analyze and use data strategically for evidence-based policy making and planning.[15]

Drawing on its experience in developing dashboards for monitoring progress toward universal health care, in Davao in the Philippines, ADB offered to develop a set of dashboards in East Java, to make data from districts available and accessible in a visually attractive

---

[11] Republic of Indonesia Act Number 14 Year 2008 Public Information Disclosure Act. http://ccrinepal.org/files/documents/legislations/12.pdf.

[12] A.G. Maail. 2018. Understanding Barriers in the Implementation of the One Data Policy in Indonesia: Insights from Health Data Journey Modelling. *ITU Journal*: ICT Discoveries, Special Issue No. 2, https://www.itu.int/en/journal/002/Documents/ITU2018-9.pdf.

[13] Indonesia Open Government Partnership 2018–2020. https://www.opengovpartnership.org/wp-content/uploads/2019/01/Indonesia_Action-Plan_2018-2020.pdf (accessed 20 June 2020)

[14] ADB supported the Kinerja project in East Java from 2016 to September 2017, succeeded by Kinerja Open Government Partnership, which was implemented from June 2018 to March 2020. Governance reforms among others included introducing a local complaint mechanism and service charters for health and education facilities, establishing community-based organizations (multi-stakeholder forums), capacity development for local governments on service standards, planning, and budgeting and trainings for service delivery units on staff attitudes towards patients in health facilities. ADB 2017. *Kinerja Jatim ADB: Consolidating and Replicating Innovative Service Delivery Practices in Districts in Indonesia–Progress Report 4 and Final Report.* Consultant's Report. Manila (TA 9017-REG). https://www.adb.org/sites/default/files/project-documents/49242/49242-001-tacr-en.pdf; ADB. 2020. *Indonesia: Improving Access and Use of Information through Open Government for Better Service Delivery and Development Outcomes in East Java* (Subproject under TA 9017 and TA 9288). Manila.

[15] Multi-stakeholder forums were established during the Kinerja project and consist of a wide array of representatives ranging from community leaders, youth forum, village youth, religious youth, civil society organizations, university, and media.

and easy-to-understand way for different local stakeholders, thereby contributing to localizing the SDGs.[16]

Leveraging Data Visualization Tools to Inform Local Policy Dialogues and Sustainable Development Goals Localization

Visualization of population data on dashboards is an innovative way that is both content-rich and easy to understand. It can support local governments to use data for more targeted interventions, evidence-based decision-making, monitoring, and awareness-raising campaigns. Dashboards can serve as a platform to combine information from disparate sources, providing the same information to different actors. Thus, they can establish a common understanding to advance cross-sector collaboration. As such, dashboards are a promising tool for participatory multi-stakeholder engagement processes and enable the public to hold local governments accountable.

A major issue of concern to the East Java provincial government were the high rates of child marriage in certain pockets of the province, as high as 30% in some districts.[17] Official prevalence data were available at districts and subdistricts, but local governments lacked data from districts to better understand the drivers of child marriage and services needed to tackle it in their constituencies, monitor progress toward eliminating child marriage, and support other local government efforts to meet the SDG 5.3 target of ending child marriages.

Child marriage is driven by multiple interwoven factors. It is culturally and locally embedded and can only be successfully tackled using genuinely intersector, local solutions. In Indonesia, district governments are responsible for services such as health and education. As such there are avenues for this level of government to address child marriage. However, they can only do this when they have access to information such as where and why the problem persists. Once they have these, they can then review their programs and policies and develop appropriate awareness campaigns.[18]

For these reasons, child marriage was chosen as proof of concept of local dashboards that will improve access to information and inform local policy dialogues to support localization of SDGs. The project aimed to improve the availability, analysis, and usage of data on child marriage, and efforts to eliminate it in the Lumajang and Pacitan districts in East Java. It is proposed that the methodology for developing local dashboards on child marriage could also be used for other local development challenges.

The project built on the Kinerja program and used the same national consultant team to allow for continuity with regard to the relationships developed with the provincial and district agencies.

A Locally Owned Process for Data Visualization

The dashboards were developed through a systematic and consultative capacity-building process to build local ownership from the onset. This process ensured local interpretation and ownership of the data and dashboards and fostered cross-sector collaboration.

Through a series of workshops, consultations, and mentoring sessions with district office staff and other stakeholders, a six-step over-all dashboard development process (Figure 3) was taken to:

---

[16] ADB. 2016. *Monitoring Universal Health Coverage in The Western Pacific: Framework, Indicators, and Dashboard.* https://www.adb.org/sites/default/files/publication/203926/uhc-western-pacific.pdf.

[17] United Nations Children's Fund. Child Marriage in Indonesia. https://www.girlsnotbrides.org/wp-content/uploads/2016/11/UNICEF-Indonesia-Child-Marriage-Factsheet-1.pdf.

[18] In Indonesia, overall, 11% of women aged 20-24 are married before the age of 18, and Indonesia has an estimated 1,220,900 child brides. UNICEF. BADAN PUSAT STATISTIK. BAPPENAS. PUSKAPA. *Child Marriage in Indonesia.* https://www.unicef.org/indonesia/sites/unicef.org.indonesia/files/2020-02/Child-Marriage-Factsheet-2020.pdf.

Figure 3: Six-Step Over-all Dashboard Development Process

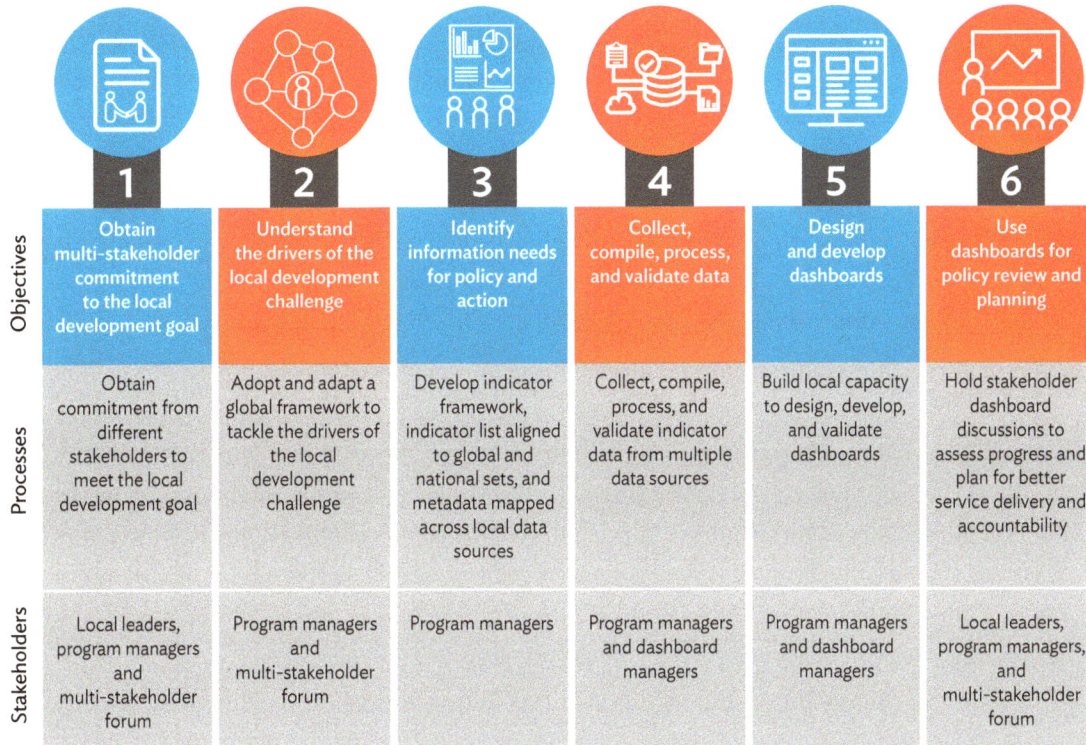

	1	2	3	4	5	6
Objectives	Obtain multi-stakeholder commitment to the local development goal	Understand the drivers of the local development challenge	Identify information needs for policy and action	Collect, compile, process, and validate data	Design and develop dashboards	Use dashboards for policy review and planning
Processes	Obtain commitment from different stakeholders to meet the local development goal	Adopt and adapt a global framework to tackle the drivers of the local development challenge	Develop indicator framework, indicator list aligned to global and national sets, and metadata mapped across local data sources	Collect, compile, process, and validate indicator data from multiple data sources	Build local capacity to design, develop, and validate dashboards	Hold stakeholder dashboard discussions to assess progress and plan for better service delivery and accountability
Stakeholders	Local leaders, program managers and multi-stakeholder forum	Program managers and multi-stakeholder forum	Program managers	Program managers and dashboard managers	Program managers and dashboard managers	Local leaders, program managers, and multi-stakeholder forum

Source: Authors.

- reiterate stakeholders' commitment to ending child marriage;

- adopt a framework to tackle the drivers of child marriage;

- identify indicators to meet information needs for progress monitoring, policy action, service delivery, and awareness raising;

- compile validated indicator data;

- design and develop dashboards for effective data visualization; and

- disseminate dashboards and use data contained in them to inform policy making, service improvement and awareness raising activities.

In addition, the process also facilitated compilation of lessons learned, discussions on ensuring sustainability by collecting data routinely and updating the dashboards more regularly, and discussions on their application for other development outcomes and SDG targets.

The Indicator Framework Development

A suitable and relevant indicator framework for the given local context needs to be developed to serve as basis for a strong monitoring support and accountability tool that would systematically assess progress toward achieving development outcomes such as the SDGs. Where possible, such a framework should use available indicators and guidance from the national level and adapted locally. Mapping indicators across all monitoring and evaluation domains—from inputs to impact—helps to better understand causal linkages, assess the availability and reach of related programs, and decide on the resources and inputs required. The domains are: Impact, Outcome, Output, Process, and Input.

While outcome and impact indicators are typically readily available, this is not the case for input, process, and output indicators. However, these indicators are crucial for local governments to understand their contributions to higher level targets and inform planning, budgeting, and policy making for SDG implementation at the local level. This is an important lesson for localizing SDGs.

The indicator framework for ending child marriage with a focus on girls in East Java was developed based on the Girls Not Brides conceptual framework to tackle the drivers of child marriage (Figure 4).

The indicator framework (Figure 5) comprises actionable indicators identified through a stepwise, logical approach across the monitoring and evaluation

domains, from inputs to impact. The indicators in the framework were further grouped by main type of program (i.e., youth empowerment, reproductive health, and education) as outlined in the Girls Not Brides framework. As a result, it is possible for policy makers and service providers to monitor and assess the availability and reach of existing services to empower the youth, improve reproductive health knowledge, and ensure secondary education.

The impact indicator is aligned to SDG 5.3.1. The reference SDG target 5.3.1 is: *"Proportion of women aged 20-24 years who were married or in a union before age 15 and before age 18."* This has been adopted in the National Socioeconomic Survey (SUSENAS) and prevalence data is reported up to the district level.

Outcome indicators were mainly adopted from the Girls Not Brides indicator set, and then reformulated according to local needs.[19]

Input, process, and output indicators were developed by the local district office staff and program managers to align with local information needs and data

Figure 4: Girls Not Brides Framework to Tackle Child Marriage

Empower girls
Provide safe spaces for girls to learn about their rights, build their confidence, and interact with their peers

Provide services
Provide educational and reproductive health services as well as legal support to girls

Work with communities and families
Work with parents, religious and traditional leaders, and men and boys to change their attitudes toward women and girls

Advocate for better laws and policies
Call for stronger legal frameworks that set 18 as the age of marriage and protect girls' rights

Source: Girls Not Brides. Girls Not Brides.org. https://www.girlsnotbrides.org/

---

[19] Aspen Institute. 2015. *Recommended Indicators for Girls Not Brides Members Working To Address Child Marriage.* https://www.girlsnotbrides.org/wp-content/uploads/2015/08/GNB-Full-List-of-Indicators_August-2015_Final.pdf.

Figure 5: Simplified Indicator Framework for Ending Child Marriage

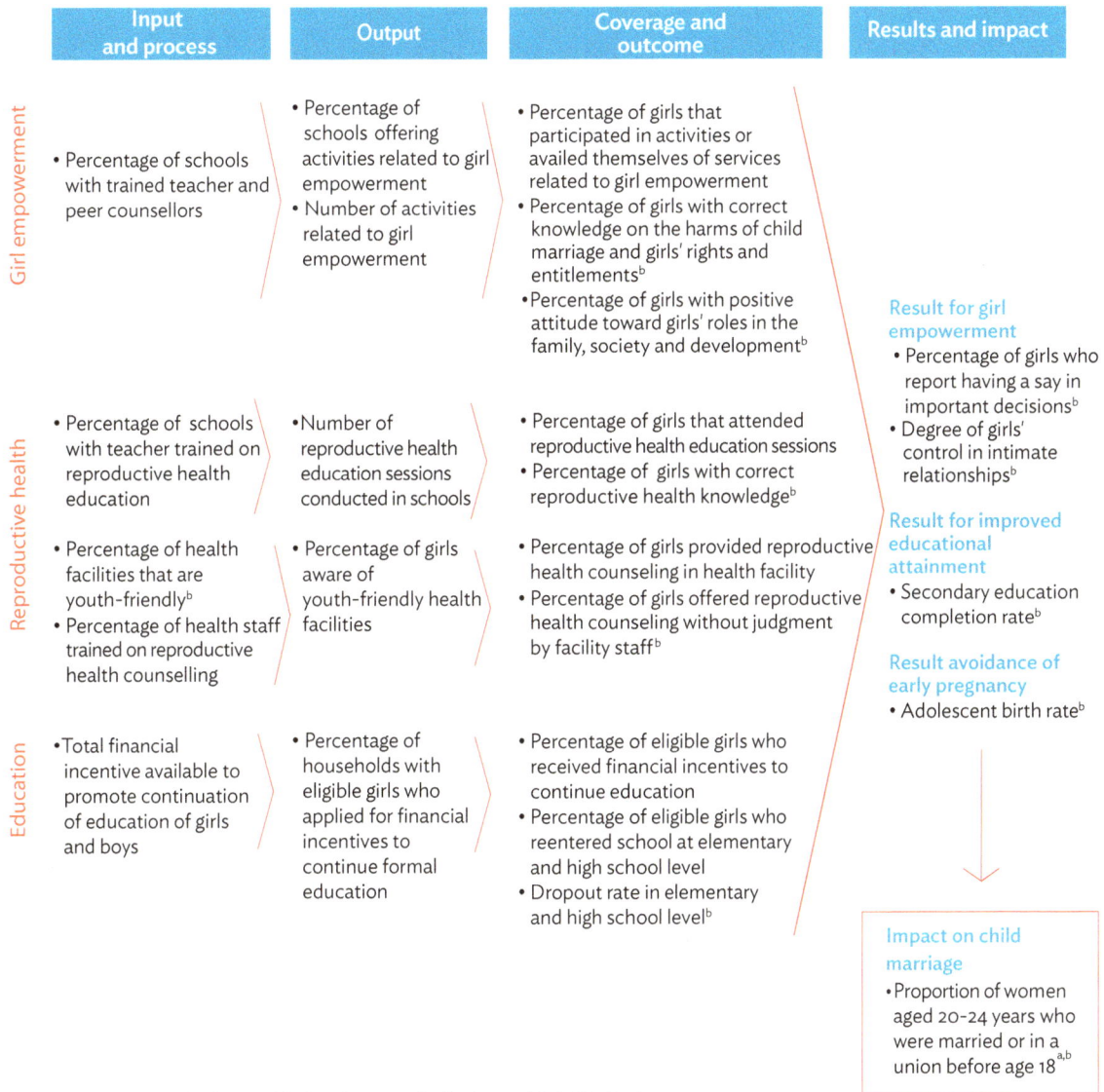

Input and process	Output	Coverage and outcome	Results and impact
Girl empowerment			
• Percentage of schools with trained teacher and peer counsellors	• Percentage of schools offering activities related to girl empowerment • Number of activities related to girl empowerment	• Percentage of girls that participated in activities or availed themselves of services related to girl empowerment • Percentage of girls with correct knowledge on the harms of child marriage and girls' rights and entitlements[b] • Percentage of girls with positive attitude toward girls' roles in the family, society and development[b]	**Result for girl empowerment** • Percentage of girls who report having a say in important decisions[b] • Degree of girls' control in intimate relationships[b]
Reproductive health			
• Percentage of schools with teacher trained on reproductive health education	• Number of reproductive health education sessions conducted in schools	• Percentage of girls that attended reproductive health education sessions • Percentage of girls with correct reproductive health knowledge[b]	**Result for improved educational attainment** • Secondary education completion rate[b]
• Percentage of health facilities that are youth-friendly[b] • Percentage of health staff trained on reproductive health counselling	• Percentage of girls aware of youth-friendly health facilities	• Percentage of girls provided reproductive health counseling in health facility • Percentage of girls offered reproductive health counseling without judgment by facility staff[b]	**Result avoidance of early pregnancy** • Adolescent birth rate[b]
Education			
• Total financial incentive available to promote continuation of education of girls and boys	• Percentage of households with eligible girls who applied for financial incentives to continue formal education	• Percentage of eligible girls who received financial incentives to continue education • Percentage of eligible girls who reentered school at elementary and high school level • Dropout rate in elementary and high school level[b]	**Impact on child marriage** • Proportion of women aged 20-24 years who were married or in a union before age 18[a,b]

Indicator source legend: [a]Sustainable Development Goal indicator, [b]Girls Not Brides.

Source: Authors.

availability, and with existing programs and services. District officers and program managers had expressed a need for information on the availability, quality, reach, and results of programs and services to tackle the drivers of child marriage.

Data Mapping and Compilation

Metadata for each indicator was also developed as a reference to outline the indicators' basic and statistical elements. This includes the indicator name, numerator, denominator, disaggregation, and the most appropriate data source. Based on this, the different data sources to populate the framework indicators were identified and mapped. Given that development outcomes are interlinked to different sectors, data needs to be sourced from multiple sources to build a comprehensive and holistic picture of the local development challenge.

Child marriage is the outcome of multiple interlinked drivers and child brides are likely to be subject to multiple intersectional disadvantages. Therefore, local data on the prevalence of child marriage and on the availability, reach, and results of programs and services to tackle its drivers had to be compiled from across a variety of sources across sectors. This was a tedious but important task.

Routinely available data from various sources related to services for tackling the drivers of child marriage had not been previously consolidated at districts. Data had to be requested from the data collection points (schools, subdistrict offices, district offices, provincial branch offices, branch national office) across different

sectors. There were instances where data were available from focal point persons but not recorded in any reporting form (e.g., number of teachers trained). As such, one of the lessons learned by the district offices was the need to develop or update existing reporting forms for regularly compiling data for selected indicators.

Data on the prevalence and trend of child marriage were gathered from the National Socioeconomic Survey through the local statistics office. Data on the causes of child marriages were provided by the Religious Court.[20] Data on services provided and service coverage came from the program databases of the local women's empowerment office, health office, education office, social office, and religious office. Data on financial assistance for continuing secondary education was derived from the program database of the local social office. Data on students' knowledge and attitude toward child marriage and gender norms, level of reproductive health knowledge, students' information sources, and their participation in activities related to protective programs of child marriage were taken from an in-school survey (Figure 6).

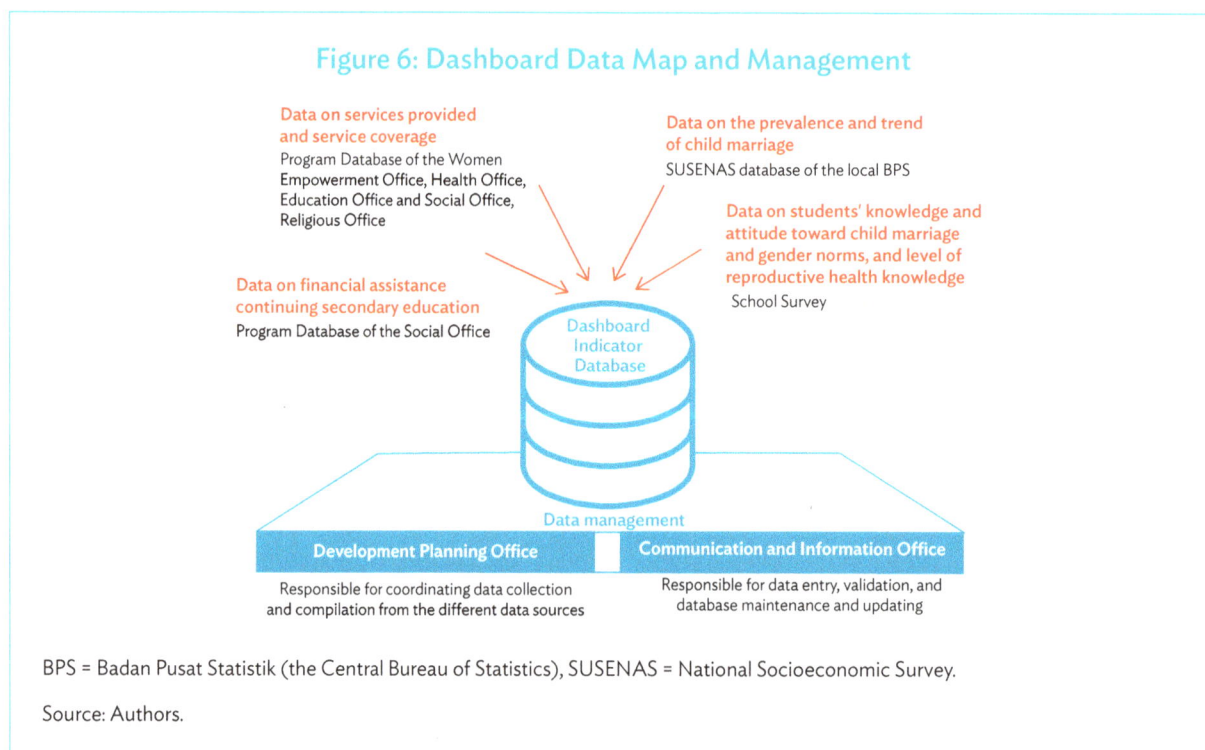

Figure 6: Dashboard Data Map and Management

Data on services provided and service coverage
Program Database of the Women Empowerment Office, Health Office, Education Office and Social Office, Religious Office

Data on the prevalence and trend of child marriage
SUSENAS database of the local BPS

Data on students' knowledge and attitude toward child marriage and gender norms, and level of reproductive health knowledge
School Survey

Data on financial assistance continuing secondary education
Program Database of the Social Office

Dashboard Indicator Database

Data management

Development Planning Office	Communication and Information Office
Responsible for coordinating data collection and compilation from the different data sources	Responsible for data entry, validation, and database maintenance and updating

BPS = Badan Pusat Statistik (the Central Bureau of Statistics), SUSENAS = National Socioeconomic Survey.

Source: Authors.

---

[20] The Religious Court is responsible for granting dispensation (exemption) process (the District Court for non-Muslims), which allows marriage with no minimum age. Otherwise the legal age of marriage is 21 without parental consent and above 19 with parental consent. UNICEF. BADAN PUSAT STATISTIK. BAPPENAS. PUSKAPA. 2020. *Child Marriage in Indonesia.* https://www.unicef.org/indonesia/sites/unicef.org.indonesia/files/2020-02/Child-Marriage-Factsheet-2020.pdf.

Dashboard Development

After data was compiled against the indicators, the different data related to child marriage were simplified and visualized through a series of dashboards (Figure 7).

Careful deliberations between local district leaders and program managers ensured agreement on the purpose of the dashboards and the intended audience of these tools: local leaders and program managers (for data-driven policy and programmatic actions including program planning and refinement), civil society, multi-stakeholder forums, and the public (for accountability and awareness raising). These in turn guided the design of dashboards and the dashboard themes and contents.

The dashboards were designed to convey key messages related to ending child marriage and tackling its drivers, and highlighted information useful for policy and programmatic actions. Some of the indicators initially laid out in the indicator framework were tweaked when dashboards were developed to transform data into information and not all indicators were used in the dashboards.

Dashboards were developed to show the trend of child marriage prevalence over recent years, and to provide information on services provided by the district women's empowerment, social, health, and education offices targeted at empowering youth (especially girls), equipping them with the correct reproductive health knowledge, and ensuring that they complete secondary education. The dashboards also reflect the outcomes of these efforts. Indicators and data on the dashboards show programmatic targets and latest status of progress, and are presented in a concise, easy-to-understand manner through the thoughtful use of charts, icons, and color schemes. The dashboards support data drilldowns to provide more granular and locally disaggregated data.

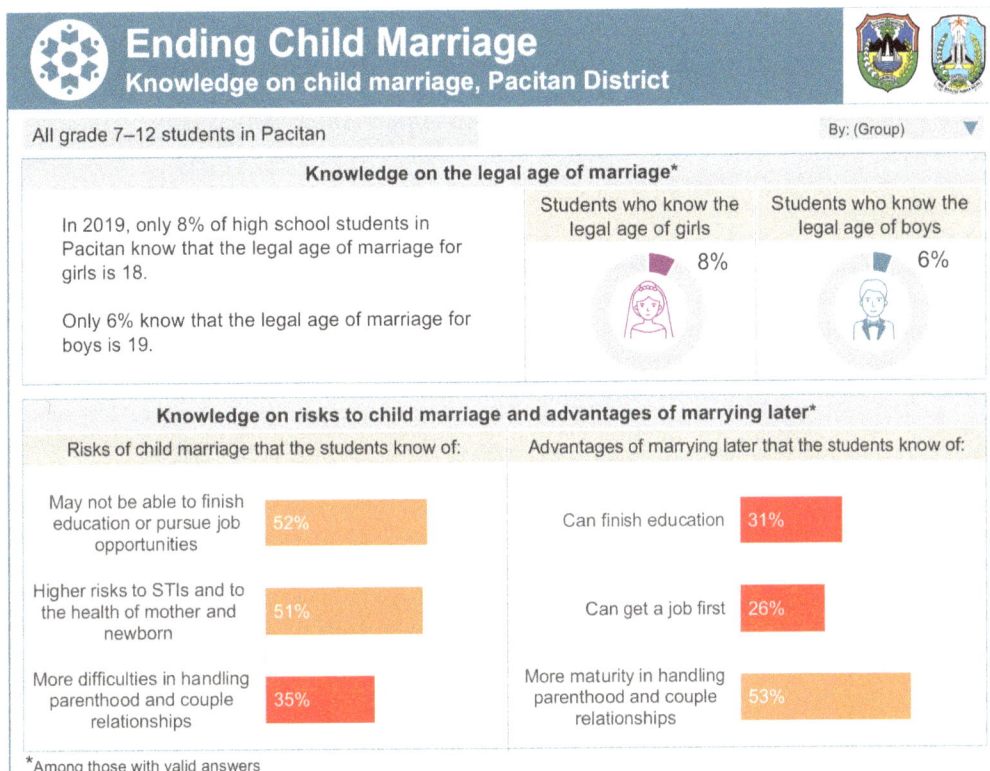

Figure 7: Child Marriage Dashboard Examples

continued on next page

Figure 7: *continued*

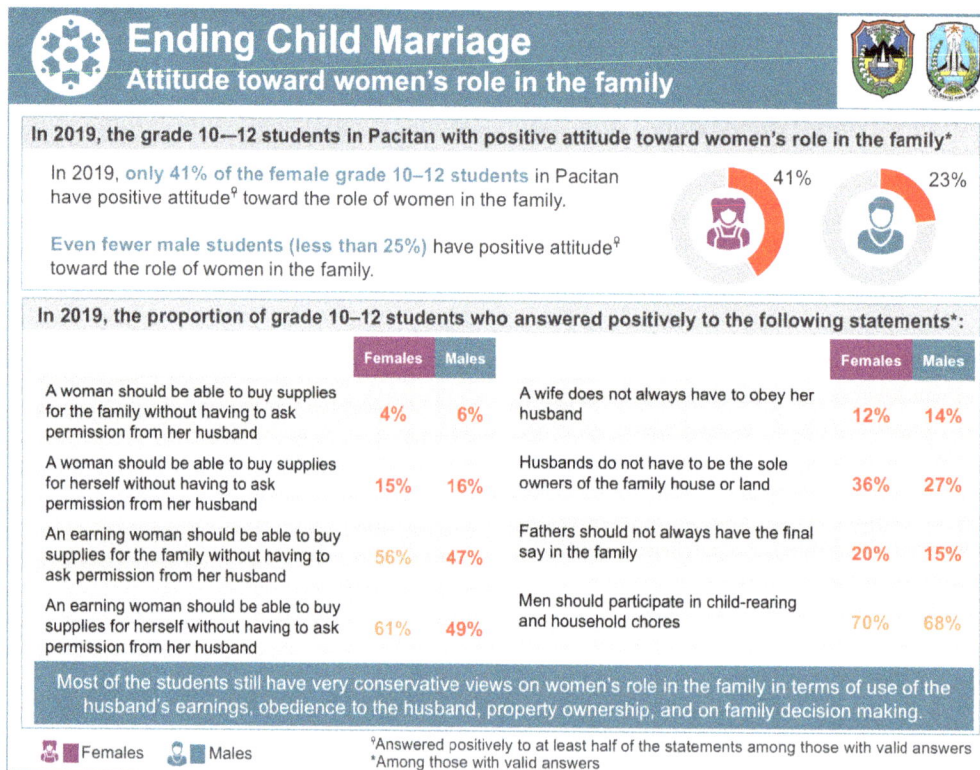

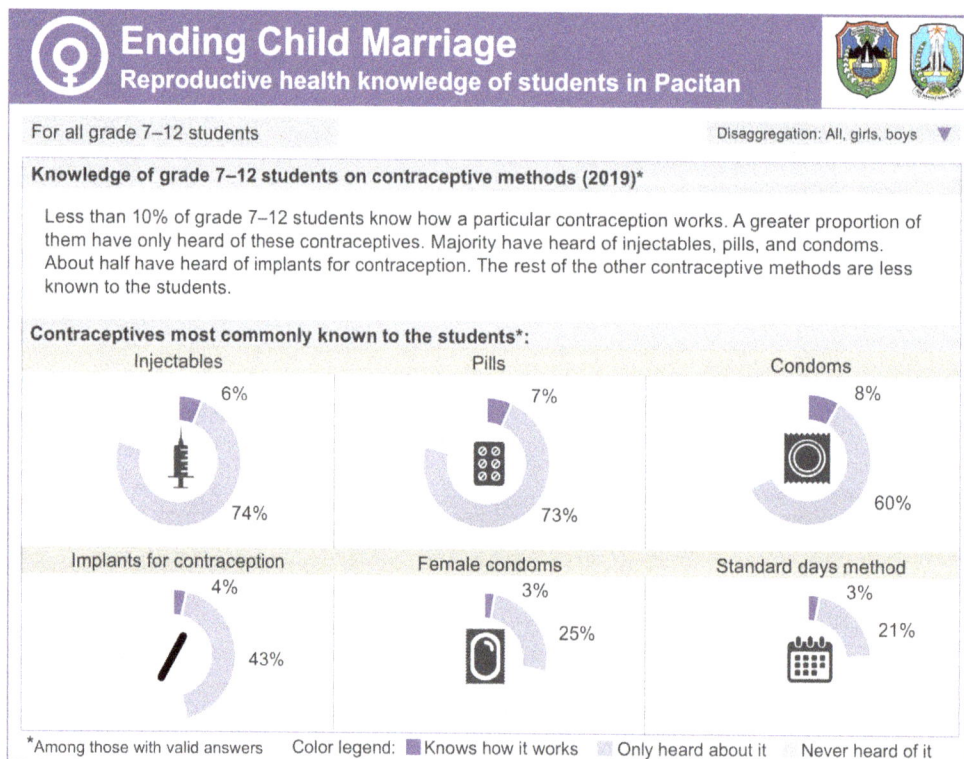

Ending Child Marriage
Attitude toward women's role in the family

In 2019, the grade 10—12 students in Pacitan with positive attitude toward women's role in the family*

In 2019, only 41% of the female grade 10–12 students in Pacitan have positive attitude[9] toward the role of women in the family.

Even fewer male students (less than 25%) have positive attitude[9] toward the role of women in the family.

41%   23%

In 2019, the proportion of grade 10–12 students who answered positively to the following statements*:

	Females	Males		Females	Males
A woman should be able to buy supplies for the family without having to ask permission from her husband	4%	6%	A wife does not always have to obey her husband	12%	14%
A woman should be able to buy supplies for herself without having to ask permission from her husband	15%	16%	Husbands do not have to be the sole owners of the family house or land	36%	27%
An earning woman should be able to buy supplies for the family without having to ask permission from her husband	56%	47%	Fathers should not always have the final say in the family	20%	15%
An earning woman should be able to buy supplies for herself without having to ask permission from her husband	61%	49%	Men should participate in child-rearing and household chores	70%	68%

Most of the students still have very conservative views on women's role in the family in terms of use of the husband's earnings, obedience to the husband, property ownership, and on family decision making.

Females   Males

[9]Answered positively to at least half of the statements among those with valid answers
*Among those with valid answers

Ending Child Marriage
Reproductive health knowledge of students in Pacitan

For all grade 7–12 students   Disaggregation: All, girls, boys ▼

Knowledge of grade 7–12 students on contraceptive methods (2019)*

Less than 10% of grade 7–12 students know how a particular contraception works. A greater proportion of them have only heard of these contraceptives. Majority have heard of injectables, pills, and condoms. About half have heard of implants for contraception. The rest of the other contraceptive methods are less known to the students.

Contraceptives most commonly known to the students*:

Injectables	Pills	Condoms
6% / 74%	7% / 73%	8% / 60%

Implants for contraception	Female condoms	Standard days method
4% / 43%	3% / 25%	3% / 21%

*Among those with valid answers   Color legend: ■ Knows how it works   Only heard about it   Never heard of it

continued on next page

14

Figure 7: *continued*

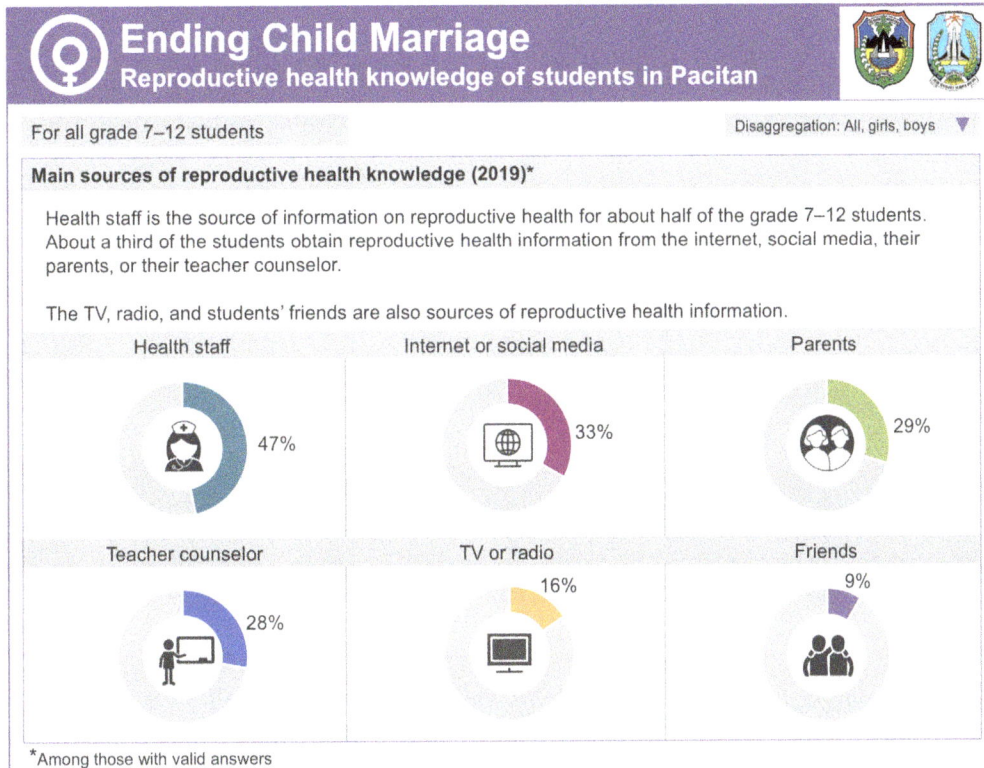

Ending Child Marriage
Reproductive health knowledge of students in Pacitan

For all grade 7–12 students

Disaggregation: All, girls, boys ▼

Main sources of reproductive health knowledge (2019)*

Health staff is the source of information on reproductive health for about half of the grade 7–12 students. About a third of the students obtain reproductive health information from the internet, social media, their parents, or their teacher counselor.

The TV, radio, and students' friends are also sources of reproductive health information.

Health staff	Internet or social media	Parents
47%	33%	29%

Teacher counselor	TV or radio	Friends
28%	16%	9%

*Among those with valid answers

Source: Authors.

15

Dashboard Use and Launch

To make the dashboards accessible to a wider audience, they were publicly launched in Pacitan and Lumajang districts on National Health Day and published on the district governments' websites.[21] Capacity development on the use of dashboards has been provided to district governments and program managers as well as village leaders, local media, and other local stakeholders.

Capacity Development for Multiple Stakeholders for Sustainability

There was a high degree of participant ownership, and the entire process was conceived as a form of capacity development for local government officials and other local actors. Creating a dashboard was a consultative process, giving participants the language and conceptual framework to have conversations with each other about a cross-sector issue, and identify the indicators and related data they each need to take action on.

Local government officials from different sectors, data clerks, and representatives from multiple stakeholders were trained to develop an indicator framework; map data available across different sources to populate the indicators; design, develop, and disseminate the dashboards; and jointly analyze the data presented to discuss the programmatic and service delivery improvements needed. Further, trainings were implemented for local media, universities, and other nongovernment stakeholders in the use of dashboards.

The following district offices were trained in developing dashboards:

- District Planning Office (Bappeda)
- District Health Office
- District Education Office
- District Women's Empowerment Office
- District Communications Office
- Local Ministry of Religion Representative Office: Local Religious Affairs Office Section
- District Social Affairs Office

Provincial government officials (from the Provincial Development Planning, Provincial Health Office, Provincial Communication and Information, Population Control, Women Empowerment and Child Protection) were consulted during the planning phase and invited to the last workshop.

Although the main objectives were the finalized dashboards and making data on child marriage more easily accessible to local governments and the public, each step in the process had its own intrinsic value. The process generated a better understanding of the issue, each actor's role, and how to jointly address it. The conceptual indicator framework gave district officials more insight into the complex dynamics of child marriage and its drivers. At the same time, it also provided capacity development on the process of making data more available and accessible, which can be replicated for other sectors and other SDGs.

The capacity development workshops on dashboard development were complemented by similar support on the use of data for different stakeholder groups, which included district and village level government staff, civil society organizations, and local media.

---

21 The dashboards are accessible at: http://dashboard.pacitankab.go.id/ (for Pacitan) and https://data.lumajangkab.go.id/?p=dashboard_p_anak (for Lumajang).

Strengthening Local Cross-Sector Policy Dialogue

Making data available and accessible is only going halfway: data can be a better catalyst when it is embedded into processes that allow data analysis and effective use. Child marriage, for example, is an issue that requires multiple sectors' responses and data related to the drivers of child marriage are usually located across different databases. The dashboard development process for the first time brought together people from health, planning, religious affairs, education, and girl empowerment (Figure 8). The dashboards equip the relevant district offices with vital baseline data about how they are performing on the drivers of child marriage and better understanding about how the services they provide should contribute toward ending it.

When the dashboards were being developed, local governments in East Java had already made significant advances in improving local governance. The Kinerja project had institutionalized a series of interventions to strengthen social accountability. This led to stronger local policy dialogues across government, communities, and service delivery actors to inform even more effective and evidence-based interventions and appropriate policy responses.[22] The Kinerja project created an enabling environment through which data could be channeled.

People-driven data drawn from the complaint handling mechanism have already been analyzed regularly by community representatives, service delivery units, and local governments to jointly find solutions—in this case, to health and education service delivery. However,

district-level data from various other sources located in multiple government departments and service delivery units was rarely systematically compiled and used to inform local policy dialogues and find solutions to pressing development challenges. There was agreement that systematic compilation and use of district-level data from various data sources could be of enormous value to improve local policy dialogues, especially when combining this data with people-driven data.

Overall, through the process of creating the dashboards, there was a growing understanding that working within one sector was not sufficient.

Cross-sector policy dialogue also supports the interconnected nature of the SDGs. Working toward policy coherence by working more effectively across sectors and levels of government is also an explicit goal in the SDGs. SDG 17 ("Strengthen the means of implementation and revitalize the global partnership for sustainable development"), target 17.14, calls on countries to "enhance policy coherence for sustainable development" as a means of implementation. The target speaks to the interconnectedness among the 17 SDGs.

Representatives from the multi-stakeholder forums were present in all the workshops and added their community perspectives. They helped improve the dashboards from a nongovernment perspective. Separate, tailored capacity development training on the use of data in the dashboards was also provided for nongovernment stakeholders, media, and academia.

---

[22] These interventions included the institutionalization of a complaint handling survey, set up of multi-stakeholder forums, capacity development for service providers, and local governments to be more responsive and accountable. The results were remarkable in that they led to significant visible service delivery improvements in health and education.

Figure 8: Working Toward Policy Coherence Across Sectors

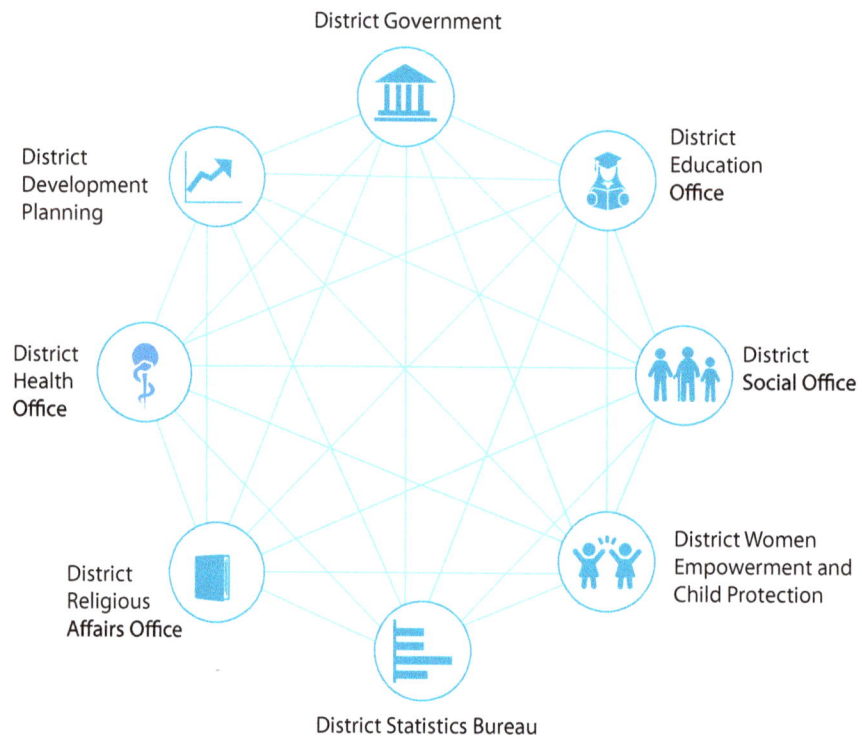

District Government

District Development Planning

District Education Office

District Health Office

District Social Office

District Religious Affairs Office

District Women Empowerment and Child Protection

District Statistics Bureau

Source: Authors.

How Presenting the Data Led to Change

By reviewing the results and outcomes on the dashboards from different services that tackle child marriage, district program managers were able to identify required service improvements, including staff training, better program development, and more targeted interventions. The dashboards revealed several facts local stakeholders were previously not aware of, such as students' poor knowledge of reproductive health issues, and the dropout rates of girls. A series of workshops on data use for different stakeholders (including local governments, civil society, and media) helped them to better use data presented in the dashboards for different purposes such as local planning, budgeting and decision-making processes, and awareness campaigns.

Several new recommendations to tackle child marriage emerged from using the dashboards, ranging from improving service delivery to awareness-raising activities. They included training teachers, counselors, peer educators, and peer counselors on reproductive health. Reproductive health materials were developed for use during extracurricular activities. Primary health care centers offered more youth-friendly activities to support girls' empowerment. Leveraging the data dashboard work led to a request for, and development of, a simple and practical manual on reproductive health and how to raise awareness and campaign to eliminate child marriage.[23]

Discussions on tackling child marriage were integrated into local planning processes. A series of integrated activities on ending child marriage was discussed and drafted during an evidence-based policy making,

planning, and monitoring workshop. These ideas were used during the districts' 2020 annual development planning process for deciding program activities on ending child marriage efforts in the following years.

The district of Pacitan further used their skills in developing dashboards to monitor the COVID-19 outbreak. This was listed as one of seven innovative COVID-19 responses from Indonesia.[24]

Training for other stakeholders, such as village leaders and multi-stakeholder forums on using the data in the dashboards to support eliminating child marriage, resulted in further ideas for tackling child marriage. For example, there were proposals on changing village regulations to prohibit child marriage. In Pacitan, the dashboards showing the prevalence of child marriage drew participants' attention to the villages with the highest prevalence rates. Facing this situation, they proposed a competition scheme between the villages with the highest levels of child marriage, with an incentive to receive funds for local development from the village fund, if there was no more child marriage.

Local media and civil society organizations were trained in using mass media and social media to raise awareness. A competition on promotional material on ending child marriage was held in both Lumajang and Pacitan. Short films, posters, and comics on child marriage were developed by young people to encourage them to become involved in campaigning against child marriage. The products will be used by the district and civil society to campaign against child marriage.

---

[23] Government of Indonesia, Lumajang Regency. http://lumajangkab.go.id. Manual uploaded to Lumajang LG's Google Drive at https://drive.google.com/file/d/10gtJTkngcUL9-ygW5jrxFlFl34JPeRkT/view. Pacitan government website: http://pacitankab.go.id. Manual uploaded to Pacitan LG's Google Drive at https://drive.google.com/file/d/10gtJTkngcUL9-ygW5jrxFlFl34JPeRkT/view.

[24] Organisation for Economic Co-operation and Development. Observatory of Public Service Innovation. COVID-19 Innovative Response Tracker. https://oecd-opsi.org/covid-response/.

The University of Jember branch Kab. Lumajang conducted their community program by selecting the Ending Child Marriage theme in Ranupane village, that has a high rate of child marriage. In addition, social campaigns were also conducted by stakeholders, such as in Islamic Group recitation, Church Youth meeting, Child Forum Conference, and also in East Java Women Islamic Organization (Muslimat NU Jatim).

Next Steps and Lessons Learned

Next Steps

Participants in this project have pledged to continue the use of dashboards to review achievements toward eliminating child marriage and program results to tackle child marriage. Increased interest of local and provincial governments toward child marriage led to incorporation of child marriage research questions and progress indicators in the replication of community complaint handling mechanisms.

The districts will be developing standard operating procedures on regularly updating the dashboards. The district governments are now considering dashboard usage for other indicators, such as education of out-of-school-youth, monitoring of COVID-19 incidence, and for other sectors. They have budgeted for the needed dashboard software in next year's district budget. Further, training of trainers is planned for the dashboard development teams trained under the pilot for potential replication in other districts.

Lessons Learned

- Local leadership is of prime importance, and so is cross-sector collaboration, multi-stakeholder engagement, and trust.

- East Java has made a commitment to improving human development indicators. It was the availability of data that made it possible to have a more in-depth conversation about early marriage.

- Access to data makes local policy dialogues more relevant to actual needs and is key to localizing the SDGs.

- Localizing SDGs by using the open government approach is effective. It allows multiple stakeholders to better understand reality, engage in a consultative process early-on, and contribute to achieving set goals.

- By using the dashboards, most stakeholders understand the content and substance faster. Usually, data is published in a scientific manner, which is not easy to understand for everybody.

- Simple is good: it is best to integrate data collection in routine systems and develop dashboards that are easy to understand.

- It is both necessary and feasible to bridge digital technology solutions with good local governance and service delivery for social justice.

www.ingramcontent.com/pod-product-compliance
Lightning Source LLC
Chambersburg PA
CBHW040147200326
41519CB00035B/7623